politically incorrect
golf Shots

JACK PALMER

summersdale

Summersdale Publishers Ltd
46 West Street
Chichester
West Sussex
PO19 1RP
UK

www.summersdale.com

Printed and bound in China

ISBN: 978-1-84953-128-3

Substantial discounts on bulk quantities of Summersdale books are available to corporations, professional associations and other organisations. For details contact Summersdale Publishers by telephone: +44 (0) 1243 771107, fax: +44 (0) 1243 786300 or email: nicky@summersdale.com.

politically incorrect
golf Shots

JACK PALMER

Illustrations by Mark Wood

contents

introduction

Golf is the only addictive thing I have ever heard of that is good for you, with all the walking, the swinging of clubs and the fresh air. The things I love about golf are the companionship of your weekend four-ball, the challenge of club and inter-club competitions, the satisfaction of smashing a drive down the middle of the fairway, chipping in or holing a long putt – and the fact that by midsummer you've got one brown hand and one white one. The list is almost endless.

Most of all, the thing I love about golf is the banter and laughter that is to be had out there on the course with your fellow players. If it is true that laughing is good for you, most golfers I know should live to a ripe old age. It is this banter and the general golf slang which inspired me to write this book of politically incorrect golf shots. In the mid-nineties I heard the first ever politically incorrect shot, named after the lovely Sally Gunnell, and since then many more such phrases have come into common use.

This book is a light-hearted record of some of the most popular phrases attributed to certain types of golf shot, illustrated to show how they appear and occasionally annotated with suggestions of how to prevent them happening to us out there on the course. No one can rule them out, so when they do inevitably occur it is amusing to refer to the particular shot with one of these phrases and have a good chuckle amongst your group of players.

I would like to dedicate this book to my fellow members at Harleyford Golf Club and all my friends on The Glen Jerry Invitational Tour.

Jack Palmer

The Long game

The Paula Radcliffe

'Didn't make it to the ladies''

Traditionally in men's golf, the penalty for this abhorrent shot is a circuit of the tee box with your trousers round your ankles. This practice is still frowned upon at some high-brow courses, particularly on the first tee in view of the clubhouse. Even if local rules forbid the obligatory circuit of the tee box, a Paula Radcliffe does garner much amusement amongst playing partners and leaves the golfer with a red face as he takes his second shot from behind the ladies' tee. To avoid this, check your fundamentals (grip, stance, posture and aim) and swing with a smooth tempo to a balanced finish.

The Sister-in-Law

'You're up there, but you know you shouldn't be'

Some days you're out there on the golf course and you can't help but think that if you didn't have bad luck, you wouldn't have any luck at all. A Sister-in-Law, in the context of golf, is something you can thoroughly enjoy: a bad shot that ends up on the green. Finally, some good fortune to reward all your hard work out there on the course.

The gerry adams
aka The martin mcguinness

'Playing a provisional'

What's worse, facing up to the fact that the first ball might be lost or unplayable and taking three off the tee just in case, or being faced with the unenviable choice of playing shot-and-distance from the straw or an ignominious walk back to the tee box to play a lonesome third shot with a hostile gallery looking on and muttering about slow play? Either way, playing a provisional will make you wish you had brought your balaclava!

In an ancient Chinese proverb, 'Confucius once say, "Golfer must play second ball first."' These days, as you barbecue your Gerry Adams down the middle of the fairway, the contemporary proverb tends to be: 'Why couldn't I do that the effing first time?!'

The Tiger Woods

'Drove off, hit a tree and found water'

Fortunately this rarely happens, but when it does it's very painful and embarrassing. Correct attribution is key: was it because of something you did wrong that you shouldn't have? Something to reflect on perhaps, as you penetrate the nineteenth hole.

The george michael
aka The grace kelly (princess grace)

'Should have taken the driver'

We all rue the public display of timidity in playing an iron off the tee when there is a relatively open fairway ahead, which is then compounded as the 'safety shot' spoons off into the boondocks or balloons up and barely makes it past the ladies', turning a par four into a par five. If there's room to spare get the Big Dog out, grip it and rip it.

At least if you are wielding the Chief when you fluff it you will go down as a failed hero as you tee up your Gerry Adams and have another go. For what it's worth, I say step up to the plate, get some distance and get away from the gallery.

The Princess Diana

'Shouldn't have taken the driver'

It's always tempting to take the Big Dog out and try to smash the ball down a tight chute, a shortish fairway, or even cut the corner off a dog-leg, but it can be a perilous decision if there's not much room for error.

Whilst I'm an ardent proponent of the Big Stick being used wherever possible, discretion is sometimes the better part of valour in tight situations (just don't end up with a Grace Kelly).

The Michael Jackson
aka The Jacko

'Started well, but faded badly'

The old golfing adage is that 'You can talk to a fade, but a hook won't listen', thereby indicating that a fade such as the Jacko is preferable to a hooking draw. This is because a fading ball loses distance and stops quickly compared to a hook, which goes considerably further once it lands due to the direction of over-spin imparted to the ball, thereby increasing the chances it will finish up in the *crap*. What is generally thought to be best is if you can repeatedly hit a straight shot with just a touch of draw, as this type of shot will be of the optimum length and yet still under control. This abortive golf shot is sometimes named the New Labour, i.e. 'starts off on the left and then curls wickedly to the right'.

The arthur Scargill
aka The jimmy Hoffa

'Great strike, but a poor result'

There is nothing you can really do about this one – if your aim was correct and you pured the shot, then it's just bad luck that took you down. It's the way it goes in golf – you know that Member's Bounce you had that won you the match on the eighteenth last weekend? This is the balancing payment going out to the Karma Bank.

The BlOnDie
aKa The marilyn mOnroe

'A fair crack up the middle'

Everyone likes one of these. Keep them coming.

The ravi Shankar

A sound-a-like for what is probably the most feared golf shot ever: the dreaded shank, which can destroy the confidence of even the most able golfers.

There's seemingly no easy solution to this problem as it is so difficult to correctly attribute the cause. We all know that a shank (or a 'Lucy Locket') comes off the hosel of the club, firing it off at a sharp tangent to the target line straight out of the socket. Often people are under the misapprehension that they're standing too close to the ball, when in fact they're too far away.

I will never forget playing at Balcomie Links in Scotland at a friend's stag weekend. I was going along very nicely for the first few holes and then, inexplicably, the Ravi Shankars started and that was it – I couldn't have hit a cow's arse with a banjo for the rest of the round.

The irish sniper

'Rick O'Shea'

Many a golfer's taters have been severely rattled as a result of an Irish Sniper, and some virtually turned into a cyclops. Very nasty indeed.

A good friend of mine, faced with a ball lying a few yards behind a tree about 150 yards out from the green, decided to go for a drawing slingshot round the trunk. Unfortunately, he must have hooded the club too much, because he yanked it straight at the trunk and the ball fired back wildly and cracked him in the 'Scotch eggs' on the full toss. He never saw it coming because he had instinctively closed his eyes as his club struck the ball (in case it came back in his face) and it wasn't until we had let three groups through that he could carry on with the round.

The Lee Harvey Oswald

'Shooting from the grassy knoll'

When the golf ball is below your feet there is a tendency for the ball to cleave off to the right (for a right-handed golfer). Conversely, if the ball is above your feet it will often yank to the left. This needs to be allowed for in the aim and striking of the ball to avoid a horror shot.

The Lorena Bobbitt

'An agonising slice that costs you a lot of length'

If you tend to fade/slice/cut the ball off the tee and you are faced with danger down the right (for a right-handed golfer), then allow for the expected slice by aiming to the left by a reasonable degree. Sod's Law often dictates that the ball hoons straight left and you wind up in the cabbage – but at least you're still in play, with your manhood intact. Some days you can appear to have been possessed by a demonic Lorena Bobbitt and you end up 'serving cake all day', slice after slice after slice.

The Michael Barrymore

'Dead in the water'

This killer shot inevitably costs you a penalty and a lost ball, and usually results from under-clubbing or fatting the shot. Take plenty of club, stay tall and swing with a smooth tempo to a balanced follow-through – these actions should avoid any horror stories.

From time to time when you hit your ball into a water hazard it's referred to as a Red October, i.e. 'it's under water and you'll never find it'.

The TONY BlAiR
(LONG game VeRSiON)

'Nasty lie'

We all regret the mistakes we make where we end up in a horrid situation that is difficult to get out of. Any attempt at finesse to recover from our mistakes is likely to be punished. So open your stance and the clubface and strike just behind the ball with considerable force and strong wrists, aiming for the nearest point of safety. It's similar to a buried bunker shot, the aim being to strike steeply behind the ball and literally blast it out of trouble.

The amy winehouse

'Over-clubbed'

A common cause of over-clubbing is when you play at an unfamiliar course that uses flagsticks which are shorter than normal, thereby making the greens look further away than they actually are. In which case, it is all the more important to trust the distance markers and the shot-saver.

Although I'm a keen believer in clubbing-up in general, sometimes the penalty for an Amy Winehouse is so heinous that it's not worth the risk, so it's better to leave it a bit short and have plenty of green to work with.

At our course there's a par four with a horrendous bowl of crap over the back of the green, the so-called Devil's Cauldron, where many a scorecard has been tarnished following an over-exuberant second shot. This shot is less well known as the Rik Waller, i.e. 'one club too many'.

The matt o'connor

'Ended up on the roof'

Thank your good fortune you didn't hit anyone or smash a window, so no harm done – you can settle into the nineteenth and enjoy the amusement of the moment.

Back in my hacking days I once thraped a nine iron from a hundred yards out. The ball went way over the green, faster than Batman down a zipwire, cracked a couple of tiles on the roof of a neighbouring farmhouse, before ricocheting over the roof line into their yard. Somewhat puzzled by my hitherto-unseen length with a nine iron, I then discovered, as I put it back in the bag, it was actually an upside-down six. This mistake is sometimes referred to as the David Beckham, i.e. 'chose the wrong club'.

The James Dean
aka The Marc Bolan

'Hit a tree and died'

This is the unfortunate result of what could have been a great shot. It's quite a common problem: you're having a good round and you're on a closing hole, you grip down and bream your driver off the deck on a par five to get maximum distance and keep it below the tree branches. You know you would have made the apron for two, if not the green, but it hits a fairway tree stone dead. You bleat to your playing partners about 'If this..., if the other...' My mantra for this sort of situation is, 'If my aunt had bollocks, she would be my uncle.' You've just got to suck it up and carry on.

The Barnes Wallis

'Bouncing bomb'

Some say 'Forget the water is even there', although for many people this refrain just makes them think about it even more, causing them to hit the water and blow up. The main thing is not to let it worry you. Check your fundamentals, take plenty of club and swing with a smooth tempo. This shot is also known as the Ted Kennedy, i.e. 'driving into the water and hopping straight back out again'.

I saw a friend of mine top his ball off the tee and onto the water. Due to the excessive top-spin, the ball skipped three or four times across the lake and landed on the fairway on the other side. I was already well down in the match at the time and when I saw this supreme stroke of luck I knew it was pretty much a lost cause.

The abU HamZa

'A nasty hook'

This is often the result of having an iron grip, so check your fundamentals (neutral grip, good stance, posture and aim) and swing with a smooth tempo. Also, if you're repeatedly hitting these snap- or duck-hooks, try taking two or three practice swings with just your left hand/arm before addressing the ball. Whilst this seems an odd thing to do, it discourages the muscling of the club through the ball with the right hand/arm which often creates this horrendous quacker of a shot, sometimes known as a mallard.

The Saddam Hussein
(Long game version)

'Loads of hang time'

It's always nice to give it the 'Billy Big Nuts', bream one down the middle and have plenty of hang time for people to admire your superior length. It's particularly gratifying from a raised tee where you benefit from even more distance and extra air time.

As juniors we used to see who could get the most hang time up on the range, with the 'holy grail' being a full ten seconds in the air. We found the best way was to tee the ball up way high, off the left toe and then give it an almighty schlap with the driver at a steep launch angle. It's a good hoot, although you have to be wary of ugly deflections that can threaten other range users. Also, it's virtually impossible to achieve a ten-second hang time with standard range balls so it's worth pulling out some cruddy old balls that you found in the rough.

The Lolo Ferrari
aka The Dolly Parton

'Big top'

A big top like this is usually caused by trying to give it the beans, i.e. taking an unnecessarily big old smash at the ball, as if to fire it out of a cannon. What you're looking for is 'effortless power, not powerless effort' – so to cure this problem stand tall and stay tall, club up and swing smooth. Let the club do the work, as they say.

Sometimes this shot is referred to as a Circus Tent, i.e. 'a big top' (albeit of a different kind).

The Lord mountbatten

'Blew up on the water'

The tighter and more annoyed you get when playing a course with lots of water, the more likely you are to blow up. Try your best to remain confident that you will strike the ball well, trust in your swing and club up to make sure you can carry the water with ease.

A great friend of mine shot his first ever eagle on a par five at a first division course in the Midlands and then on the next par five did a Lord Mountbatten and carded a Laurel & Hardy – ten, i.e. a thin one (1) and a fat one (0) – after blowing up on the water.

The John rambo

'Hit a branch on the way down'

Going over an obstacle, particularly from close quarters, is a high-risk, high-tariff shot. We've all gone for the Hero Shot over a tall tree and failed to make it, with the ball looking as though it's over and then striking a branch on the way down, ruining what you expected to be a great shot. Either that or you power-blade the ball straight into the woodwork. Unless you're really on your game and are confident of a pure shot, a chip-out to safety or a low punch- or chop-shot under the branches are worth considering.

The elephant's arse

'It's high and it stinks'

It could be the ball is teed up too high or you've got a fluffy lie; either way, you go under the ball and it goes really high but not very far. On the tee box, tee the ball down a bit. In the case of a fluffy lie, stand tall and stay tall – sweep the ball off the grass, nice and smooth.

On a sheltered driving range the classic, audible sign of an Elephant's Arse is when you're happily in the zone and suddenly there's a god-awful clang as some plonker goes under the ball and hits the roof, shattering your concentration. This abortive shot is sometimes known as an Angel Gooser, or a Regi Blinker (rhyming slang for a 'real stinker').

The Kate Winslet

'A bit fat, but otherwise perfect'

On occasion you unwittingly over-club and end up fatting the shot slightly. Then you realise, as the ball ends up on the green, that a pured shot would have sent you long.

The Kate Moss
aka The Bobby Sands

'A bit thin'

The phrase 'thin to win' is often heard on the golf course when someone accidentally hits a thin shot and it ends up on the green or close by. Whilst many a thin shot can be disastrous, firing the ball over the back of the green into a world of hurt, low crop-dusters that are just a bit thin can often work well. 'Thin to win' should only be viewed as a conciliatory comment when you mishit a shot; taking more ball is usually better. This shot is sometimes known as the Morgan Fairchild, i.e. 'pretty, but just a bit too thin' or, in the event the ball doesn't travel very far, the Posh Spice, i.e. 'too thin and not enough legs'. Furthermore, a thin shot that travels too far, like a power-blade, is sometimes known as the Peter Crouch, i.e. 'too thin and too much legs'.

The robin cook
aka The george mallory

'Died on the hill'

When you're playing uphill the golf hole is effectively longer, and on an up-slope the club you're using becomes more lofted; therefore, go up a club or two and make sure you get all the way up to the flag. Conversely, on a down-hill lie the club effectively becomes less lofted and therefore the ball flies further. As a rule of thumb, every four degrees of up- or down-slope equates to another club either way. For an extreme example, on a forty-degree up-slope from a hundred yards out, a shot that would normally need a wedge would, in theory, need a one iron.

The Steve McQueen

'Great escape'

Thank your lucky stars and move on.

I'll never forget watching golf on TV and seeing Tiger muller his ball with an iron from right behind a pine tree. He hit a low punchy draw that worked out perfectly. The fact that he wrapped his club round the tree and nearly fell over as he walked off didn't detract from the shot at all – it was a proper Steve McQueen.

The Danny DeVito

'Short, fat and ugly'

Often caused by trying to murder the ball and sometimes referred to as a 'ground-breaking ceremony' if conducted on the first tee, this shot usually results in a divot the size of a wig going further than the ball, a rather red face and a sore wrist. To cure this, go through your normal pre-shot routine to reduce tee box nerves and swing with a smooth tempo to a balanced finish.

A few years ago, a friend performed the worst Danny DeVito I've ever seen, hitting the AstroTurf mat at the driving range with tremendous force: as the ball slowly rolled off the front of the driving bay the severed head of his three wood hit the corrugated iron roof with an ear-splitting bang. The club head and the jagged stump of shaft ricocheted into the next booth.

The SONNY BONO
aka The Michael Kennedy

'Hard and fast, straight into the trees'

The Sonny Bono, similar in result to a James Dean, is a true horror shot that occurs when you bream the ball straight into the woodwork. It could be poor aim or a bad strike; either way it's best avoided, lest you end up being beaned by a deflection or wind up in a deadly lie.

The O. J. simpson

'Got away with it'

Bank it and move on, just don't push your luck – or next time you could wind up in serious trouble.

The Ken Livingstone
aka The nancy pelosi

'A long way left'

Different to a duck hook or quacker, this pull shot can be caused by poor aim, a glancing blow off the heel of the club or more often by coming across the ball and dragging it left. It's important to work on your pre-shot routine so that you naturally set up with the correct aim and position in relation to the ball. Envisage the correct shot before you strike it and swing with a smooth tempo and maintain good balance. If you keep pulling it despite these corrective measures, it's worth trying two or three practice swings just with your left arm (as with the Abu Hamza) before driving the ball off the tee. This shot is sometimes also known as the Mickey Mantle, i.e. 'a dead yank'.

The rubber johnny
aka The condom

'It was safe, but it didn't feel great'

Sometimes you have to put safety first to ensure you stay alive.

The Jean-Marie Le Pen
aka The Sarah Palin

'A long way right'

There are quite a few potential causes of a Jean-Marie Le Pen: poor aim, a slice, a block, very strong side wind, even a toe-er or a shank. Correct attribution and then relevant adjustment is key. The best thing to do is take your normal stance, perform your pre-shot routine and then swing with a smooth tempo without trying too hard to manufacture a shape which is unnatural for your swing.

For me, in the past, the most frequent cause of this mistake was trying too hard to draw the ball which would often block it out straight right or produce a ballooning slice. Occasionally, instead of blocking or slicing the ball, I would double-cross it, which creates a duck hook. This problematic condition is sometimes known as the Ru Paul, i.e. 'a slice that turns into a hook'.

The Vinnie Jones

'A nasty kick when you're least expecting it'

The opposite of a Member's Bounce, this is always unfortunate and often seems to happen when you've had a great front nine and just talked your score up at the turn – thus becoming heavily over-drawn at the Karma Bank and finding yourself caught by the short and curlies soon thereafter, usually on the tenth or eleventh hole.

Whilst I maintain that it's bad luck to be superstitious, we've pretty much banned the talking-up of each other's front nine scores at the turn in case we put a hex on our friend's back nine. It's all very well if someone wants to talk up their own score, and when newcomers do it we nod sagely to each other as the wheels come off soon afterwards, in the knowledge that they have invoked the dreaded tommyknockers once again.

The Mole Shagger
aka The Worm Burner

These are terms for a long, low shot that skids and bounces along the fairway – 'shagging moles' and 'burning worms' as it goes.

This shot tends to be caused by the player not getting enough of the ball, i.e. they've thinned or bellied it, imparting top spin which can give the ball surprising distance and sometimes ends in a reasonable result.

Occasionally, a similar type of shot, particularly off the tee, is referred to as the Bruce Forsyth, i.e. 'a big chinner', as the ball literally comes off the chin of the club which delivers a low shot with characteristic top spin and rather poor penetration.

The John Travolta

'Stayin' alive'

It is always a relief to have the good fortune of a John Travolta out there on the course. Just be extra careful of the next shot because all too often if you get lucky one moment, you'll cancel out that good luck by cleaving the next shot into trouble. Aim away from the danger to allow for an extra margin of error.

I've seen playing partners over the years calling dubious 'rabbit scrapes' or 'staked tree' to get a favourable drop and then promptly hooning their ball into even worse trouble. If you've got a legitimate drop then make the most of it, otherwise it's best to take your medicine and put safety first.

The Dick Cheney

'A wild and wayward shot'

It is vitally important to take careful aim at your target before taking your shot, lest you accidentally blast someone. Occasionally, someone who keeps hitting Dick Cheneys on a round is temporarily dubbed 'Buckshot Billy', as he sprays shots all over the place.

Many years ago we were hacking round a 'goat farm' in Berkshire and my mate schmoked a Dick Cheney off a raised tee with poor aim but loads of distance, right over the next fairway. The ball eventually descended behind a clump of bushes, there was a distant 'CRACK' and some guy, who had been lurking behind the bushes, came scuttling out looking around furiously to see who had hit his trolley. Fortunately we were too far away for him to realise it was us and we all had a good laugh, although in retrospect a hearty old 'roar of the fore' would have been wise.

The russell crowe

'Big, but a bit fat'

Often the result of trying to give it the 'Johnny Large Potatoes' on the tee box, this is usually caused by hunching in to the down-swing, thereby connecting with the ground before the ball. When this is performed with a driver or other wood it is sometimes known as the Victoria, i.e. 'a fat wood'.

A good drill, to avoid hitting the ground but still give the ball a mighty hoon, is to tee it up a bit and forward in your stance, hover the driver slightly above the ground at address and tilt your right shoulder down a bit (for a right-handed golfer). Keep the tempo smooth and make sure your left elbow doesn't break down at the top of the back swing, as over-extension will likely cause your arm to chicken-wing, resulting in an arcing slice.

The Swampy

'Went up in a tree and stayed there'

It is quite rare for a golf ball not to fall back out of a tree, although fir trees are possibly the worst culprits for this. When it happens it feels so unfair that you can't help but think, 'Surely I should get a free reload for that?'

A friend of mine drove his ball from a raised par three tee at our course and yanked it into a tree trunk full-on and it just stuck there, amidst the tentacles of ivy, for all to see and too high up to retrieve. Years on, it's still there and has since been joined by a further three tree-huggers.

The Stevie Wonder

'Playing blind'

If you're playing blind and a safety shot is not a viable
option, move to the nearest point at which you can
clearly see your target and gauge the distance and the
line from where you will be striking the ball. If you've
got an obstacle to go over, lay the club you're intending
to use on its back and carefully step on the face, thereby
raising the shaft. The angle the club shaft points up at will
indicate the trajectory the ball will follow and therefore
whether the club is lofted enough to make it over –
providing you don't fat it or skull it into the furniture!

Sometimes these shots are referred to as the Arsène
Wenger, i.e. 'everyone saw where it went but you'.

The Sally Gunnell
aka The Liz McColgan

'Doesn't look great, but runs for ever'

Basically a thin shot that works out well due to the excessive top spin generated by striking the top half of the ball, the contours and/or gradient of the fairway and weather conditions – as it says, not a great looking shot but a good worker.

Less well known as the Forrest Gump, i.e. 'it just keeps on running'.

The gorden kaye

'Heavy contact with wood'

It's a common problem this one – you try to bend a shot round a tree that's encroaching on your line of attack, thinking 'a tree is 90 per cent air', and, 'Allo 'Allo, the ball finds the one branch protruding from the foliage and fires off at an angle, sometimes resulting in negative yardage.

The Glenn Miller
aka The John Kennedy Jnr

'Didn't make it over the water'

Faced with a large expanse of water and a must-make shot, we've all topped or skulled the ball into the drink, or simply not taken enough club. All you can do is club up, take a smooth swing and think of hitting the target on the other side, as opposed to thinking of 'not hitting the water'.

At a local golf course, where I've played many a time, there's a medium length par three on the front nine with big water on the left. Here I once turned it over so badly it made it to the fairway of the previous hole and I had a half-decent pitch coming back (barring the embarrassingly long walk around the lake). In these situations it's best to tee up thinking positively about hitting the target and visualising the shot.

The russell grant

'A fat iron'

Usually a Russell Grant is the result of trying to give it too much beans, so you end up hunching into the shot and hit the ground before the ball. The prediction here is that you will observe a massive divot flying through the air in your very near future. This is the classic, abhorrent shot of a hacker and it stinks like a skunk in a gym bag.

Try to remember the all-important mantra 'effortless power, not powerless effort' and let the loft of the club do the work. Head up a bit, stay tall and ensure you're standing the right distance from the ball at address so as to maintain good balance through the swing.

The Peter mandelson

'An unbelievable iron'

There are few more satisfying shots in golf than striping a
long iron from 200 yards out and stiffing the pin.

The Douglas Bader

'Looked great in the air, but didn't have the legs'

A common mistake this one: we all like to think that we can thrape a wedge and stiff the pin from the one-fifties, but in reality it usually takes the perfect shot. Club up and swing with a smooth tempo and often as not you'll end up close.

Occasionally this type of shot is known as the Natalie Gulbis or the Anna Kournikova, i.e. 'it looks great, but it's unlikely to get a result'.

The Ladyboy

'It looks like an easy score, but all might not be as it seems'

It does happen: you're on the tee at an unfamiliar course and you shoot for the flag you can see, hole out and then realise with a nasty surprise that you've played to the wrong green. Or it looks like a clear, straight shot down the fairway, but there's a hidden ditch full of nasties and you find it. Never good.

The short game

The adolf Hitler

'Taking two shots in a bunker'

Whilst the vagaries of bunker play are such that no one can completely rule out the occasional Adolf, for a greenside bunker shot open your stance to the target, shuffle your feet down into the sand to stabilise yourself and, with an open clubface, strike the sand two to three inches behind the ball and ensure you follow through with a full swing to avoid making a complete hash of it on the first attempt.

The eva Braun

'Picked up in a bunker'

There's not a lot you can do about this one – if you've blobbed or lost the hole and you're in the bunker, best take your medicine and move on. If you're in the Monthly Medal with no blobs allowed, no Eva Braun for you.

I was playing in the Club Championship a few years ago. My campaign was already over, having taken a nine on seven, but one of my playing partners was going along quite well. A high-handicapper, he ended up in a greenside bunker off the tee on our signature par three, hole twelve. He took eight shots to get out of the sand and skulled his final bunker shot over the green into a lateral water hazard at the back. I reckon he would have welcomed the opportunity for an Eva Braun, but red-of-face he had to carry on. Always a bitter pill to swallow.

The erwin rommel

'Taking several attempts to get out of the sand'

Inevitably an Erwin Rommel starts out as an Adolf, and there are few things in golf more annoying and embarrassing than that – possibly a shank, but definitely a Rommel. The longer it goes on the worse it gets.

The true agony of an Erwin Rommel is played out in a Medal or Club Championship when some hapless player ends up in a gnarly bunker and just can't seem to get out, often finally escaping only by virtue of skulling the ball way over the other side of the green. This brings little relief to the person who has just realised their round is over and their handicap is going up 0.1 again. If anything is likely to make someone lose their cool out on the course it's a disaster like this.

The yasser arafat

'Ugly and in the sand'

Same drill as for buried lies and fried eggs – open up the stance and clubface, shuffle down in the sand and hit behind the ball with maximum force and full follow-through, aiming for the lowest part of the bunker face that you can without disturbing your swing.

The Saddam Hussein
(short game version)

'Going from one bunker to another'

Not many people have two golfing phrases dedicated to them; only Saddam Hussein, Tony Blair and Michael Jackson. This shot is also sometimes referred to as the Osama Bin Laden.

In terms of the short game meaning, the Saddam Hussein can occasionally be seen alongside the Yasser Arafat, the Adolf Hitler, the Erwin Rommel and the Eva Braun to create the truly awesome spectacle of a 'Dictators' Convention', with its sole attendee leaving the 'convention' feeling well and truly pistol-whipped.

The Honeymoon Putt

'It goes off in your hands and you miss the hole'

Calm down and take it steady. Think of something to distract you momentarily from the pressure to perform. Don't think about how firm you need to be to get it in the hole, let the subconscious do its work.

Sometimes you lose your feel on the green and keep roasting your putts way past the hole. A friend of mine, who is normally a very good putter, once in a while fires a Honeymoon Putt twice as far as it needs to go. It's become a mini tradition that someone will then mutter in their best cockney accent, 'It went orf in me 'and, Guvnor!', which is very amusing for everyone else, although I suspect it's wearing a bit thin for the chap concerned.

The Fairy queen

'A big bender that lips the rim'

This is quite a common, if infrequent problem – you stroke a long, breaking putt with lots of borrow from the far side of the green, it's curling round homing in on target, the fist-pump is already being initiated and then the ball lips the rim and is left some way out of the hole, leaving you sputtering like a candle in the wind and puckering up over the next putt.

The Cuban

'Needed just one more revolution'

As a famous golfer once said, 'I've never seen a short one go in yet,' or, as my missus says, 'You've got to be up to be in.' There are few things more annoying than stroking a great putt, seeing it roll straight at the hole and then at the last minute it pulls up just short and someone pipes up, 'Hey, unlucky mate – right street, wrong house!'

The only time I've seen a Cuban go in was when I was playing links golf at Dunstanburgh Castle. I left my ball stone dead, just short of the hole, but as I walked up for an easy tap-in a big gust of wind blew it in for me, thereby saving me a shot (it was definitely within ten seconds, honest). Shots like this are as rare as Cuban smoke in the White House.

The Bill Clinton

'Close, but no cigar (and it leaves a nasty taste in your mouth)'

Very similar to the Cuban; this is easily done, but try to give those putts the extra ounce needed to get them up to the hole.

The Monica Lewinsky

'All lip and no hole'

Also known as a Mother-in-Law, i.e. 'nothing but lip'.

The Mick Jagger
aka The Leslie Ash

'Big lip-out'

A most frustrating result to a good putt that looks like it's going in, but then catches the lip and gets fired out in a slingshot effect by gravity. This can be quite damaging on a sloping green as the ball can sometimes end up further from the hole, thereby leaving you with another knee-knocking tester to come back at.

There's not a great deal you can do to eliminate this happening, although more putting practice should help reduce big lip-outs and, as with all putts, avoid the 'poke and peek' approach – for complete satisfaction, ensure the ball has left the putter face before you look up.

The Jeremy Beadle

'Short-sided'

If you've missed the green and the flag is tight against that side of the green, particularly if it is well-defended, it's worth aiming for the heart of the green just to err on the side of safety.

I suspect it's the case with many a weekend golfer that this is one of the worst situations to find yourself in. More often than not, to pour salt into the wound, the grain of the grass is against you or you're in a tight lie on a spot of hard pan. The temptation is to go for a spectacular flop shot, but this requires a near-full swing and if you thin it you're in Hurtsville. If you've got the room, then, it's best to go for a chip-putt or, if not, then a standard pitch with a high degree wedge; you could even stun it into the bank and let it pop up onto the green.

The Lindsay Lohan

'Ended up in the hole and popped straight back out again'

Also known as a Doughnut Puncher, i.e. 'made the hole and came straight back out again', these often occur on those pesky winter greens when you give the putt a good tonk across the uneven surface – it goes in and then comes straight back out again, having hit the top of the inner cup and bounced back. Sometimes a golf ball is declared 'scared of the dark' and is peremptorily smashed into the jungle as a pre-emptive warning to other errant golf balls that might choose to misbehave.

As an example, a foursomes-playing partner and I once had the ball in the cup three times on one hole. He hit a punch shot from a hundred yards, it bounced once, hit the pin, dropped straight down into the hole and then bounced right back out again. I putted it in too firm and it came back out again, then he finally put it out of its misery, the two of us turning what could have been a heroic eagle into a disappointing par.

The Chilli Dipper

'A fiery one'

So called because the ball comes out 'red hot', Chilli Dippers are caused by skulling the ball and can result in anything from broken clubhouse windows and shattered roof tiles to superficial injuries. To avoid this, make sure you hit your pitch with conviction and think 'hit all the ball' as opposed to 'don't thin it', because the subconscious cannot be correctly programmed with negative thoughts.

When practising around the chipping green, make sure you're not diametrically opposed to someone trying out their lob shots, because sooner or later they're going to chilli dip one right at you and there's no time for a 'FORE!'. This shot is also known as a power-blade or, in less severe cases, a flyer from the chip shop. A further permutation is known as the Wilfrid Brambell, i.e. 'a thin iron'.

The Linda Lovelace

'Drained a long one, straight down the throat'

Feels good, doesn't it?

The Cutty Sark

'Well and truly roasted'

Sometimes you've legitimately got to give the ball a good roll to have the best chance of saving a hole in a match (or for a point in Stableford format). If it misses it inevitably finishes quite far from the cup, but at other times your touch and feel seem to desert you and you start roasting your putts way past the hole. It's a perplexing development in anyone's game, but the trick is not to try to over-think your shots as you could then start oscillating between roasters and twitchers: one minute long, the next minute woefully short.

This can be the start of the yips, where you lose all touch and feel on the green. Try to forget about the last dodgy putt and just play each one as it comes. Take a deep breath, double-tie the old 'balloon knot' and loosen your putting grip.

The rock Hudson

'Thought it was straight, but in the end it wasn't'

Sometimes you read a putt as being straight to the hole and then on its way it veers off due to an unforeseen gradient in the slope of the green. All you can do is try to improve your green reading, possibly by looking at it from both ends if there is time, to try to smoke out any illusory undulations.

At my home course, there's a general rule of thumb that all putts borrow towards the River Thames and it is proven true time and again, even to the point of putts appearing to break uphill and defy gravity. Visitors to our course can be quite perplexed by this phenomenon, although physics suggest it is probably an optical illusion since it's highly unlikely you would observe a ball actually breaking up a slope.

The gerald ratner

'Well plugged'

In damp, muddy conditions you can sometimes find that the ball plugs into the soil where it lands, either on or off the green – particularly when the ball has flown really high and then plummets back to Earth. Generally you are allowed to take relief from a plugged ball, unless it's a fried egg in a bunker in which case there's nothing that can be done about it.

The Brazilian
aka The gynaecologist's assistant

'A very close shave around the lip'

Often the putted ball appears to cross a cellophane bridge and everyone on the green is astonished that the ball didn't drop, leaving the player incredulous and bleating about how unfair it was. Sometimes it's just a straight rim burner – quite painful, like the morning after a vindaloo.

The Tony Blair
(short game version)

'Too much spin'

It's very gratifying for amateur golfers when they succeed in peeling back a pitch shot even if it finishes further away from the hole, because it is perceived that a correctly struck short iron should spin back on a receptive green. Whilst always great to see, the peel-back is only of use if you've hit it past the hole in the first place. This shot is sometimes also known as a Michael Jackson, in the context of a ball that appears to 'moonwalk' across the green.

The Dennis Wise
aka The Nicole Richie

'Nasty little five-footer'

Keep the putting grip light, not enough to squeeze toothpaste out of a tube. Pick a small target, see the line and let the putt roll to the hole. Try not to think too much about pace, let your subconscious do the work. It's for these sort of putts that it's best not to get into the habit of giving and accepting too many generous gimmes in friendlies, because when you are in the Monthly Medal you'll tend to tweak most of them, costing you 0.1 on your handicap.

The King Tut
aka The Devil's Stovepipe

'Buried in the sand'

As with all buried lies and fried eggs in bunkers, you have to really give it a ladle of chilli beans, but ensure you strike the sand a good margin behind the ball to blast it out, concentrating on finishing the full swing – avoid the short, stabby hack that will leave you up against the face for another awkward shot and a guaranteed Adolf, possibly a Rommel.

The term Devil's Stovepipe was originally given to sites where ancient trees have toppled over and become buried in sand. Over the ensuing centuries the core trunk of the tree decomposes leaving a bark shell and a hollow tube beneath the sand. Unwary hikers, walking across the sand, can suddenly fall into the void and the fragile walls of sand then collapse, burying the hapless walkers in a deadly morass of sand from which they never escape. Even more soul-destroying than wrecking your Medal card in a pot bunker, I should think.

The andy mcnab

'Double tap'

The Andy McNab, also known as a Double Chen after Tze-Chung 'two chips' Chen, often happens in the bunker or around the green and usually results from a nervy, stubbed chip followed by a scoop. What can you do? Suck it up and carry on, but make sure you hit those short chips with conviction and follow through properly on those bunker shots.

The worst Andy McNab I know of is when a friend at my home course chunked his bunker shot, hit the ball again on the follow-through and stood there looking around, wondering where the ball had gone. It had gone up high from the double tap, then it came down, hit him on the head and glanced off the sand wedge he was holding, thereby costing him four shots and leaving him in the bunker for another go.

The Salman Rushdie
aka The James Joyce

'A very difficult read'

Often called a snake, these multiple break putts are very tricky indeed. It is best to first ascertain whether the whole green itself is sloping one way or the other as that will provide the overriding borrow on the putt. Then all you can do is try to work out how the undulations will affect the line of the putt and trust in your subconscious to make the best of it. Sometimes you can concentrate so hard your eyes hurt, but you still can't get a good read.

Sometimes such very difficult putts (and other testing shots) are referred to as the Robert Downey Jnr or the Kerry Katona, i.e. 'a real snorter'.

The Hannibal Lecter

'A fast approach with lots of bite'

This is a useful shot to have in your armoury, particularly if the greens are hard and fast. By hitting down on the back of the ball with a lofted club you impart huge amounts of backspin. This backspin, combined with the lofted trajectory, causes the ball to bite and peel back when it lands, preventing it from rolling off the back of the green.

This shot is sometimes known as a Chubby Checker, particularly if the initial strike was on the fat side. A further variation is the Mike Tyson, i.e. 'a low punch with savage bite'.

The general Belgrano

'It's good to sink a big one like that'

Few things boost your confidence as much as sinking a big one in the clutch.

The Sphincter Winker
aka The Bum Squeaker

'A fairly short putt that has you puckering up over it'

Take a deep breath, pick your line and target and then roll the putt with conviction. Remember, if fear is the poison then let confidence be the antidote.

An enduring bugbear of mine is when you occasionally come across a green that has such a steep slope to it that a golf ball will not come to rest on that part of the green. The greenies go and place the hole in the middle of it for the day and you see people putting up the slope towards it and then the ball rolls all the way back down, then they do it again, and so on – bringing on a proper case of the old Trumpeter's Lips.

The David Trimble

'A tentative prod'

Putting can be a daunting prospect, particularly if you've not played for a while. Fast, undulating greens can intimidate the nervous golfer and result in a run of tentative prods that leave the ball woefully short of the hole and can cause a series of three-putts, or 'three-jabs' as they're sometimes referred to, which can soon derail a player's round.

There are a few well-used comments that one often hears on the green after someone has had the misfortune of a David Trimble, including 'Does your husband play?', 'Excuse me, I think you've dropped your lipstick', 'Halfway for the ladies!' and 'I think you've got sh*t on the end of your club… no, the other end!'

The best excuse to fend off any irritating jibes is to immediately claim that your putter head scuffed the ground and to ask around whether that's ever happened to anyone else, which it inevitably has. (Just make sure you give the next few putts enough gas!)

The Pee-wee Herman

'Too much wrist'

The Pee-wee Herman can apply to various types of golf shot, although it seems especially prevalent and damaging in the short game – trying to scoop the ball off the ground with a lofted club or steering a putt with an unnecessarily wristy stroke. Generally speaking, in the short game you want to take your wrists out of play for most shots.

The general game

oprah golf

'Fat, thin, fat, thin'

Oprah Golf is a distressing condition to find oneself in out on the course. It can begin with one bad shot and incorrect attribution: for example, perhaps you top a shot and someone says to you, 'It's 'cos you lifted your head up, mate.' On the next shot you focus on keeping your head well down and end up paffing a fat shot just a few yards and getting a face full of dirt spray. Then someone else says to you, 'You know what they say, "If you keep your head down you'll be looking at a big divot," haha!' Funny, but not helpful.

A friend badly afflicted with Oprah Golf one day, described it perfectly when he said through gritted teeth that his fairway woods and short irons had inexplicably turned into his 'pitching woods and driving irons' as he spooned his long fairway shots high up into the air and bladed his approach shots over the greens.

The enron
aka The Farepak Hamper

'Total collapse'

Probably symptomatic of a poor mental game or simply a culmination of bad luck on the day. Keep your chin up and keep smiling. Remember, a bad day's golf is better than a good day in the office.

A couple of years back we were four down with five to play in our weekend four-ball better ball match, standing on the fourteenth tee. Our opponents could taste victory and were busy sharpening up their tomahawks to give us a good scalping. Then, having invoked the tommyknockers with their premature and ill-advised comments, they performed the perfect Enron and we ended up winning five holes in a row and took them down to Chinatown on the eighteenth.

monkeyboy golf

'Playing in the trees all day'

We've all been there and it's usually the result of a combination of bad luck and poor shot selection. You can never rule out a visit to the tree line, but to rule out Monkeyboy Golf always think safety – sometimes even a good malleting of the ball with your putter can fire it out below all the branches and back on to the short stuff.

The ike Turner

'Giving the old bag a good slapping'

This one comes back to the mental game. If you've had a bad shot, suck it up and carry on – slapping your bag about with your club only serves to impress upon your playing partners that you've lost your grip. Stay focused and don't get tight over the ball.

I've witnessed much bag slapping in my time and, whilst quietly amusing for everyone who's watching, it's very bad form. Apart from which it can damage a perfectly good golf club. I have a friend who was playing with someone who got so mad that he went the whole hog and tried to throw his entire set of clubs, bag and all, into the woods. It fell short because of the weight and my friend couldn't resist saying, 'I think you need to take a mulligan.'

The Paris Hilton

'An expensive round'

Usually, the phrase Paris Hilton is attributed to the losing hole of a match where a decent sum has been wagered on the result. With the notable exception of our annual society comp we tend to play for beers at the nineteenth or a fiver each, thereby reducing the chance of an expensive round and keeping the stress levels down.

According to golf legend, one golfer said to his playing partner on the practice green, 'Hey mate, do you fancy playing 10p per hole, double or quits?' His partner agreed and off they went. Unfortunately, the guy whose idea it was lost all eighteen holes on the bounce and had to hand over £13,107.20. That last hole was the epitome of a Paris Hilton.

The Urologist's assistant

'Playing with another man's ball'

It is an easy mistake to make – you hoon your ball into
the Serengeti, think you've found it, play it out and then
realise to your dismay that you've played with another
man's ball. Golf being golf, most players will call foul on
themselves. A few others, I suspect, would carry on and
subtly change back to their usual brand before the
next tee shot.

The Mrs Doubtfire

'A chap who spends too much time in address'

Everyone has their own unique pre-shot routine – some take practice swings and some don't, some people woggle the club face back and forth a few times. Occasionally you will play with someone whose pre-shot routine has evolved into a very long, wiggly, twitchy, procedure of addressing the ball: hence they are a Mrs Doubtfire.

I have heard of someone who performed two dozen wiggles and woggles prior to every tee shot and some of his playing partners couldn't even bear to watch. Some people do it on the green as well, taking aeons to size up their putt, appearing to have frozen over the ball, only for the putter to eventually go off in their hands and roast the putt way past the hole. Most Hanoi-ing, as they say in Vietnam.

The Denzel Washington

'Man on fire'

The phrase 'Denzel' is a temporary mantle of honour donned with pride by a golfer who plays outstandingly on the day, as in: 'Old John played out of his skin, he was most definitely Denzel for the day.'

The alan Titchmarsh

'Hacking about in the cabbage'

How you got into the cabbage in the first place determines the advice for how not to next time, but we are where we are and it is important, particularly if the ball's sitting down in the thick stuff, not to go for the Hero Shot with a fairway wood or a long iron. If it is really nestling down, play it similar to an explosive bunker shot, i.e. open your clubface and stance and, using a lofted club, strike down steeply just behind the ball with considerable force, strong wrists and good follow-through, taking the shortest route to safety.

A legend of our annual Club Championship is one hapless member who carded a twenty-five on the second hole after driving eight balls into the mahoofka and performing a most excellent Alan Titchmarsh. He took over half an hour to clear the hole and he still had thirty-four to go.

The Lawrence of arabia

'Spent all day in the sand'

Some days you might as well take your bucket, spade and a deckchair to the course with you, as you spend hole after hole 'on the beach' – power-blading balls from one bunker over the green and into one on the other side or hacking about in pot bunkers unable to escape. It's pretty demoralising stuff. All you can do is calm down, take stock and pick targets that are well clear from the danger of bunkers.

At a local course, where they use forty tons of sand per year just topping up the plethora of bunkers, a new member accepted a £50 bet that he couldn't get his first full round in without going in at least one bunker. He played the whole round hitting eight iron after eight iron and eventually, many hours later, came into the nineteenth and claimed his winnings.

The Jabba the Hutt

'Big fat stinking blob'

When playing Stableford format, a blob is when you shoot sufficiently highly on a hole that you can't score any points. It happens quite a lot, but that doesn't make it any less annoying, especially when you string together a whole load of blobs and some dweeb pipes up and dubs you 'Mr Blobby' or the 'Blobmeister'.

The Bernard Matthews

'Missing lots of birdies'

The positive you should really take away from doing a Bernard Matthews is that at least you were on the greens in regulation to give you those realistic chances of birdies. If you keep it up the putts will start to drop before long, so whatever you do keep plugging away and don't get mad about it.

If you monitor your golf stats you will find that the more greens in regulation you hit, then generally the more putts you take. This is because if you hit a par four green in regulation from 175 yards out it's less likely to be as close to the hole than if you chip on for three, thereby making it a big ask to sink many of the putts first time. So doing a Bernard Matthews is an inevitable initial result of getting on top of your long game and one not to be too concerned about.

The robert mcgee

'Well and truly scalped'

The term 'scalped' is used in lots of sports when a player or team goes down like the Hindenburg, but probably no more so than in golf – although there are various interpretations. Mainly, a single player is scalped when someone with a significantly higher handicap shoots a lower gross score. In Match Play it is when you lose by a lot of holes, ten & eight being the full chrome-domer.

This wretched situation is named after the only known survivor of a true scalping. In 1864, Robert McGee was scalped by Chief Little Turtle of the Sioux and left for dead. I've been the victim of many a 'scalping' on the golf course, and that's quite unpleasant enough.

The Tommy gainey

'Tommy two-gloves'

Some golfers prefer two gloves, some none at all. There's no right or wrong, although 99.99 per cent of golfers stick with the traditional one-glove approach and, to an extent, the 'Tommy two-gloves' option is seen as the choice of a schmendrick (with the exception of the double wet weather gloves that provide more grip the wetter they get – a truly marvellous invention for inclement golfing conditions).

The Chinook

'Club chuck'

Named the Chinook because of the distinctive 'WHUP-WHUP' noise a golf club makes when someone loses the plot on the course and chucks it. Whilst very amusing for everyone else, it only serves to reinforce the suspicion that the individual concerned is not on top of their mental game. Best avoided if at all possible.

I know of one chap who schlapped his drive into a world of hurt and, in the ensuing fury, chinooked his club into the air and it landed up in a tree. He then thought it would be a good idea to throw his wedge up to dislodge the driver, followed soon afterwards by his seven iron. At that point a playing partner appeared with the flagstick from a nearby green and poked them down for him.

army golf

'Left, right, left, right!'

Sometimes it seems you can't get the ball onto the fairway – you pull one into the broccoli up the left and then blast it across the fairway into the leeks on the other side, then get a flier over the green and chilli dip the one coming back. There's no one easy solution to this problem, although in general if you play each shot as it comes and soldier on without self-flagellating for the miss-hit you just had, you'll cut down on the Army Golf and stay off the Bogey Train.

The Dog Licence

'Seven & six'

So named after the cost of a dog licence in the old days and used in golf when you win/lose a match seven & six – for example, 'I gave him his Dog Licence', denoting that your opponent played like a dog. Not a nice way to go down in a match, shaking hands on the twelfth green – but still, at least it wasn't a ten & eight drubbing.

The Slavomir rawicz

'Going for "the long walk" in'

Unless it is due to particularly inclement weather or physical injury, it is highly inadvisable to walk in because it displays a weakness of mental game which will be commented upon in the nineteenth after your sad and lonely departure. Instead, plaster a shit-eating grin on your face, keep your chin up, and remember – next time it will be some other bugger's turn to suffer.

Having played golf with countless people over the years one mid-handicapper immediately comes to mind. He expected every shot to be the shot of a pro and when it inevitably wasn't, he would start swearing, then club-chucking, then bag-slapping and then finally do a Slavomir and go for the 'long walk', leaving me and others bemused as to why someone would inflict this much hurt on themselves when they've come to play a game.

The Ben Hur

'The wheels came off'

The phrase 'the wheels came off' is common in golf and is applied when someone is going along well and then, towards the end of the round, everything falls apart. Whilst Ben Hur, in the 1959 film of the same name, in fact won the race and his chariot wheels didn't come off, we're all familiar with what happened to those in the race whose wheels did come off – they ended up eating dirt.

All you can do is make the best of each shot as it comes and never give up until that ball rolls into the eighteenth cup. Audible self-deprecation is a definite no-no as that will loosen up those wheels something rotten. This nightmarish development in someone's round of golf is occasionally referred to as the Payne Stewart, i.e. 'he played some great golf, but eventually crashed and burned'.

www.summersdale.com